FAREWELL, JOHN BARLEYCORN

FAREWELL, JOHN BARLEYCORN

PROHIBITION IN THE UNITED STATES

MARTIN HINTZ

LERNER PUBLICATIONS COMPANY/MINNEAPOLIS

Special thanks must be given to the librarians, museum administrators, police officers, tourism officials, authors, and historians who contributed to the research on this book; to Mike Beno, editor of *Reminisce* magazine, for his suggestions, referrals, and leads; to Alfred Epstein, librarian of the National Women's Christian Temperance Union; and to history teacher Ray White for his valuable insights and comments. And warm thanks to all the folks who lived through the Prohibition era and were willing to share their insights on a fascinating slice of American history.

Page 2: As Prohibition begins, beer is drained into a city sewer.

Library of Congress Cataloging-in-Publication Data

Hintz, Martin.
   Farewell, John Barleycorn : prohibition in the United States / Martin Hintz.
     p.   CM.
   Includes bibliographical references and index.
   Summary : Discusses alcohol consumption in colonial America, the temperance movements of the nineteenth century, and the impact that the prohibition of alcohol had on the nation
    ISBN 0–8225–1734–5 (alk. paper)
    1. Prohibition—United States—History—20th century—Juvenile literature.
   2. Drinking of alcoholic beverages—United States—History—20th century—Juvenile literature. 3. United States—Politics and government—Juvenile literature. 4. United States—Social life and customs—Juvenile literature. [1. Prohibition.] I. Title.
HV5089.H55 1996
363.4'1'0973—dc20   95–37415

Manufactured in the United States of America
1 2 3 4 5 6 - JR - 01 00 99 98 97 96

Contents

HOW DRY WAS HISTORY?

The first Pilgrim to step from the good ship *Mayflower* at Plymouth, Massachusetts, in 1620 might have raised a toast to his safe arrival in the New World. The rugged little vessel carried numerous casks of beer, wine, and gin for the difficult transatlantic journey. On long sea voyages, fresh water was hard to come by, and alcohol was a popular substitute.

Records of the first Europeans on America's mainland tell about the colonists' "great thirste" after their original supplies of European-made alcohol ran out. The settlers then turned to making their own wine. Newly arrived German immigrants often put their beer-brewing expertise to good use.

From the earliest days of America's settlement, pioneers enjoyed their occasional drink. Not only did alcohol blunt the fear and loneliness of dark, chilly nights on the frontier, but whiskey was also believed to combat a host of illnesses and injuries, ranging from snakebite to itchy scalp. Drinking was also a social pastime, indulged in whenever far-flung friends got together. Trading posts often doubled as inns and taverns. Hosts were expected to provide drinks for visitors and "one for the road." No one seemed to need an excuse to drink.

One historian noted that revelers in a Rhode Island town drank 32 celebratory toasts when the hated Stamp Act was repealed in 1766. In most colonies, work customarily stopped at 4:00 P.M. so laborers could have a drink. And "good employers" saw to it that workers always had plenty of liquor as a perk. Rightly or wrongly, alcohol was considered a benefit, a blessing, and cure-all.

Colonial still, 18th century

Some colonies had a tavern for every hundred white people. Slaves and most free blacks weren't allowed in taverns, so they weren't counted in the tally. No "respectable" woman of the era would have been seen in a tavern. But that didn't mean that women didn't drink at home. Lots of people, regardless of age, sex, and race, indulged. Even crying babies were quieted with doses of rum and opium.

Imported barley malt whiskey was rare and extremely valuable in the rough-and-tumble new country. Sometimes it replaced hard currency, which was also rare on the frontier. Homemade whiskey, distilled from corn mash, was valuable too. It was relatively easy to transport and was often exchanged for other products in eastern markets and at the port of New Orleans. Much of the better liquor was sent back to Europe to pay for goods that Americans didn't produce themselves.

A pleasant night in the local tavern

Innovative colonists made alcohol from almost anything. One song from the 1700s went like this:

> If barley be wanting to make into malt,
> We must be content and think it no fault,
> For we can make liquor to sweeten our lips
> Of pumpkins, and parsnips, and walnut-tree chips.

Another popular drink was rum, made from richly fermented West Indian molasses. The rebellious Sons of Liberty refreshed themselves with plenty of the fiery drink while planning the break with England. Patriot Patrick Henry once remarked that the local pub was the cradle of American liberty—because so many meetings were held in drinking halls. During the Revolutionary War, spirits were part of the daily rations of soldiers and sailors. Rum diluted with water was called grog, a drink popular with sailors on long voyages.

When George Washington said goodbye to the army after the war, he knew where his comrades-in-arms would be gathered. Washington's moving farewell speech was made from the steps of Fraunces Tavern in downtown New York City.

TWO SIDES TO THE ISSUE

But not everyone approved of drinking. Although the first Pilgrim might have toasted his safe landing in the New World, the second Pilgrim off the boat might have frowned on that drink. Indeed, from the earliest colonial times, there have always been supporters and opponents of alcohol.

Many Protestant groups, including the Methodists and Lutherans, had strong antidrink traditions based on biblical teachings. Drunkenness was the subject of many sermons in colonial America, with more than one minister warning against such "sundrie notorious sins." But most ministers, civic leaders, and educators pleaded for drinking in moderation rather than total abstinence (not drinking at all). That would come later.

In the mid-1600s, Governor Peter Stuyvesant tried to control the spread of "bawdy houses" (brothels—which also sold liquor), in New

Amsterdam. He was unsuccessful because the wealthy men who owned taverns in the growing settlement (later called New York) objected strenuously to any attempt to cut their profits. For a short time in the early 1700s, Plymouth officials tried issuing licenses as a way to regulate the spread of pubs. But, since so many people liked to drink, regulations were usually ignored.

In 1785, Dr. Benjamin Rush, surgeon general of the Continental army, expressed alarm at the amount of drinking done by the troops. In his pamphlet, "Moral and Physical Thermometer of Intemperance," he noted that a drunkard usually ended up in bad shape:

> In folly, it [drunkenness] causes him to resemble a calf; in stupidity, an ass; in roaring, a mad bull; in quarrelling and fighting, a dog; in cruelty, a tiger; in fetor [smell], a skunk; in filthiness, a hog; in obscenity, a he-goat.

"THE OLD MAN'S DRUNK AGAIN"

There was also a growing number of hard-core abstainers. The word *temperance* referred to abstinence from drinking. Historians peg 1808 as the start of the full-blown temperance movement in the United States. In that year, 23 people in Saratoga, New York, formed a temperance society, aiming to warn people against the perils of alcohol. In 1818, the Massachusetts Society for the Suppression of Intemperance was organized.

The first heavy volleys fired in the war between the "Drys" and the "Wets" came in 1819. In that year, the secretary of war banned the use of liquor on army posts. Soldiers could still drink off base, which many did, but the rule was a taste of things to come.

More temperance societies sprang up. By 1833, at least 6,000 local organizations opposed to drinking had formed around the country. By 1851, these groups had held four national temperance conventions. At these meetings, speaker after speaker related the terrible results of over-drinking. Some believed that drunkards could catch fire if they came too close to a lighted candle. In some cases, speakers warned, drunkards could explode like kegs of gunpowder. Or their blood might catch fire and would be seen bubbling under the skin. Preachers pointed out that these fiery displays were only a small taste of what awaited drinkers in hell.

But most conventioneers were concerned about the here and now as well. Criminals and prostitutes often hung around saloons, which were believed to be breeding grounds for disease. Many women joined the Dry cause, concerned about drunkenness and its effects on families and the workplace. Drinkers often neglected their jobs and families. Wages went to beer and whiskey instead of rent and food; drunken men were often violent toward their wives and children. One leading prohibitionist suggested:

> If there is, as there will undoubtedly be, a drunkard's family in your vicinity, you can each organize yourself into a committee of the whole for its protection, comfort and help. Perhaps the children should be removed from the dangers that are about them in a home to which a man "crazy on purpose" comes reeling out of the saloon.

***Public drunkenness
caused alarm.***

Sorrowful songs told the story. "I See You've Been Drinking Again" was one such song:

> You promised tonight you'd come sober
> And spare all my sorrow and pain . . .
> But I heard that your step was unsteady,
> I knew that my hopes were in vain,
> When you stumbled and fell in the hallway,
> I knew you'd been drinking again.

Other songs praised the drinking of water:

> It gives neither headache, nor heart-ache nor pain
> No trouble attends it, no loss but all gain.
> Hail, hail, water hail!
> 'Twill make the cheeks rosy which wine has made pale.

Visiting temperance workers asked families to "sign the pledge" against drinking.

Many women who joined the temperance cause were active in other social reform movements of the era: the drive to abolish slavery, the fight for women's rights. Temperance would improve society, the women hoped: clean up cities, strengthen women's rights in the home, and improve family life.

"RUM, ROMANISM, AND REBELLION"

More objection to drinking came from rural areas of the United States, from people who looked with fear at the explosive growth of cities and their swelling immigrant populations. Urban areas, increasingly filled with foreigners, were considered by some to be centers of depravity and drunkenness.

In a backlash against both urbanization and alcohol, many Drys ran for local office. With a strong grassroots push, Dry politicians gained control of numerous small towns and rural counties. As they grew stronger, the Drys flexed their political muscle in state legislatures. In the 1840s and 1850s, several counties and towns passed antiliquor laws. Some local regulations were very strange. In one West Virginia community, a friend could drink in a neighbor's house only if he or she didn't visit for the express purpose of drinking beer.

In 1851, Maine became the first state to totally outlaw the manufacture and sale of alcohol. Portland Mayor Neal Dow had long complained about "drinking houses and tippling shops" and had lobbied the state legislature to pass the ordinance. The "Maine Law" signaled an ominous trend in the eyes of Wets elsewhere in the country. Maine's law remained on the books for the next 70 years and was considered a model for those who endorsed total Prohibition—a nationwide ban on alcohol.

But even with the growing political power of the Drys, the liquor trade was one of the nation's biggest industries in the late 19th century. Alcohol was cheap, plentiful, and tempting to drink after—even during—work. In the 1880s, a glass of rye whiskey sold for ten cents and a pitcher of beer for five cents. Factory workers sent "pail boys" to nearby taverns to bring back buckets filled with beer.

In 1874 the Women's Christian Temperance Union was organized to

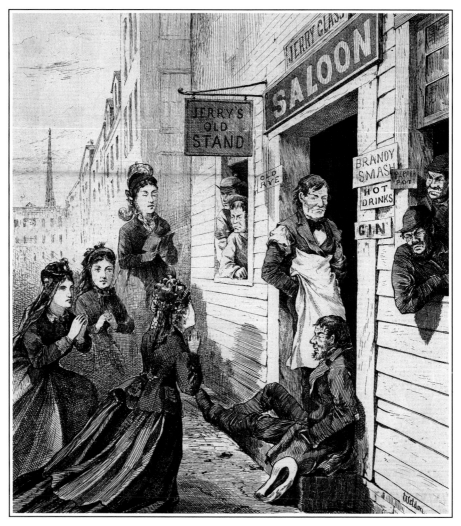

Showdown at the local saloon, 1874

combat what it viewed as a world going mad with drink. WCTU members stood outside taverns to pray and sing such hymns as "Jesus, the Water of Life Will Give." These concerts caused much discomfort to those who had retreated to the taverns for peace and quiet. But that was the whole idea. The women in these "visitation bands" didn't want the drinkers to get too comfortable.

Frances E. Willard, dean of women at Northwestern University in Evanston, Illinois, became an active member of the WCTU and eventually its national president. She was converted to the cause during a protest in Sheffner's, a bar in Pittsburgh. In her book, *Glimpses of Fifty Years,* Willard wrote of the experience:

> It was strange, perhaps, but I felt not the least reluctance . . . and kneeling on that sawdust floor, with a group of earnest hearts around me and behind them, unwashed, unkempt, hard-looking drinking men. I was conscious that perhaps never in my life save beside my sister Mary's dying bed had I prayed as truly as I did then. This was my crusade baptism. The next day, I went on to the west and within a week had been made president of the Chicago WCTU.

The saloonkeepers fought back. In Cincinnati, one threatened to turn a cannon on the protesters. Praying women were pelted with stones and garbage, even attacked by vicious dogs. One protester allegedly calmed three fierce hounds by "gently laying her hands on their heads, and as though taught of a higher power than their master's, they crouched at her feet and were quiet." Such tales became part of the folklore of the era.

The debate over alcohol eventually reached the highest levels of society and politics. During the 1884 presidential election between Republican James G. Blaine and Democrat Grover Cleveland, the Republicans blasted the Democrats as the party of "Rum, Romanism [Catholicism], and Rebellion." The tactic backfired, however, as large blocks of angry city voters—many of them Catholic immigrants who enjoyed their traditional beer and wine—went Democratic. Cleveland was narrowly elected president.

BARROOM BRAWLS

One vocal member of the WCTU, Carry Nation, would earn a place in American folklore. Nation's home state of Kansas had passed a prohibition law in 1880, but no one paid much attention to it. Many taverns operated openly, a fact that infuriated Nation. In 1899, a grim Nation stormed into a local tavern and smashed the place with a hatchet. She then crashed her way through other taverns throughout the state. Although she was arrested and jailed several times, no charge would hold. There was the thorny judicial question of how Nation could be charged for damaging property that legally wasn't even supposed to exist.

Nation's exploits continually made the front pages of newspapers and helped publicize the temperance cause. After one rampage, the grandmotherly looking woman was locked up and spent the night praying on her knees. Captured in news photographs, with a Bible at her side, Nation was the epitome of antidrink zeal.

Saloon owners, brewers, and distillers laughed at Nation. One brewer offered her $500 to smash his barrels—so he'd get the resulting publicity. Bar owners posted signs that said All Nations Welcome But Carry. Others invented vile-tasting Carry Nation cocktails, much to the amusement of their patrons.

Carry Nation spends a night in jail.

But more often, the liquor business ignored all the temperance furor—or further damaged its own reputation. Distillers and brewers sometimes raised prices illegally. They ignored laws that required the use of pure ingredients, clean bottles, and the labeling of chemicals and additives. This disregard for the public often pushed people to support the Drys, even if they didn't always approve of the Drys' tactics.

Brewers owned in part or in full more than 80 percent of the country's saloons. The Shades of Death, Mule's Ear, Hell's Half Acre, Certain Death, and Devil's Den in Xenia, Ohio, were typical. They stank. They were seldom scrubbed out and served as hangouts for derelicts, criminals, and other rough characters. Sawdust on the floor soaked up vomit and tobacco juice. The air was always hazy-gray with rancid cigar smoke.

Saloon patron, late 19th century

Brewing was a major industry in cities such as Milwaukee and St. Louis. Wets worried that Prohibition would result in lost jobs and would hurt the nation's economy.

The Anti-Saloon League of America (formed in 1895), the WCTU, and similar organizations were determined to shut the places down.

But while the Drys were gaining momentum on the local and regional levels, they hadn't yet passed any national laws. That began to change in 1903, when Drys put so much pressure on legislators that the bar in the United States Capitol building was closed. This action hit home for many lawmakers who had felt up to that point that the Drys were merely a radical fringe group. Meanwhile, more towns, counties, and states passed prohibition laws.

But whether Prohibition was the real wish of a majority of citizens has long been debated. In many elections, only a small group actually voted or could vote. During this era, women did not have the right to cast a ballot. Many African Americans were barred from voting—sometimes by threat of violence—especially in the South. And hundreds of thousands of new immigrants, many uneducated and unfamiliar with the American political system, didn't participate in elections. Often, votes for state and local prohibition laws squeaked past with just a small group of supporters.

The Drys were aware of these numbers and realized that the more forces they put out on election day, the better off they'd be. With money, clout, and emotion, they prepared for the next stage in what they saw as the battle for the soul of America: total national abstinence.

PROHIBITION WINS OUT

The saloon comes as near to being a rat hole for the working class man to drop his wages in as anything I know of. To know what the devil will do, find out what the saloon is doing.

—Minister Billy Sunday

Antidrink forces were constantly on the march in the early 1900s, spending millions of dollars. Speakers crisscrossed the country, roaring for the no-booze cause.

Between 1909 and 1912, the American Issue Publishing Company, the mouthpiece of the Anti-Saloon League, turned out 40 tons of antidrink material each month. It regularly churned out the *American*

Issue, the league's official newspaper, as well as *New Republic, American Patriot, National Daily, Scientific Temperance Journal,* and tens of thousands of charts and other documents.

All this literature pounded away at a single issue: no alcohol. Gradually, the editorials and stories became more and more political. "No . . . citizen should ever cast a ballot for any man, measure or platform that is opposed to the annihilation of the liquor traffic," said one publication. Another urged voters to "rescue our country from the guilt and dishonor which have been brought upon it by a criminal complicity with the liquor traffic."

Many Methodists and Baptists eagerly took up the cause. Pulpits were pounded, and churches rang with warnings against evil drink. On World Temperance Sunday in 1916, tens of thousands of Sunday school students signed antidrinking pledges. The children eagerly promised never to drink any kind of alcohol in their lives.

The Dry message was not subtle: drinking could lead to ruin.

The Saloon put me Here.

A VOICE FROM THE TOMB

Even some liquor interests began to look seriously at wrongs within their industry. At a meeting in 1908, the United States Brewers' Association loudly issued a statement against "dives"—the run-down taverns that stood outside the factories of many American cities and blighted neighborhoods. An editorial in *Bonfort's Wine and Spirit Circular,* a trade newspaper, lamented that the modern saloon "has been getting worse instead of better. It has been dragged into the gutter; it has been made the cat's paw for other forms of vice; it has succumbed to the viciousness of gambling; and it has allowed itself to become allied with the social evil." An official of the Wisconsin Brewer's Association blasted retail liquor dealers as "bums and beggars, not fit to associate with yellow dogs."

But all these words did little to actually slow the use of alcohol, even in communities that professed to be Dry. Stills (distilling units—bulky cookers used to process alcohol) were hidden in barns and basements. Smugglers sneaked alcohol from Wet communities into Dry ones. Drinks were served in secret, unlicensed back rooms called "blind tigers" and "blind pigs." Cops and sheriffs could be bribed to leave the places alone. Some officers even acted as enforcers or guards for illicit booze-running operations. In fact, it was often just as easy to find a drink in a Dry county as it was in a Wet one.

SHADOWBOXING SATAN

Whether they drank or not, churchgoers heard plenty of sermons on the evils of drink, especially on what was called the "kerosene circuit." This nickname referred to religious meetings held outdoors, under tents or in fields; kerosene lanterns provided lighting at night. One of the most famous ministers on the circuit was Billy Sunday.

Sunday had been a professional baseball player, and he knew how to play to the crowds. In his light gray suit, white shoes, linen shirt, and white silk tie, he was an eye-catching figure. When preaching, he threw off his coat and starched collar and jumped up on tables in front of his wildly applauding, shouting congregations. He shadowboxed an imaginary Satan and sprinted up and down the aisles as if chasing the devil.

Sunday's audiences loved the performance. Journalists liked Sunday because he always gave them wild, headline-worthy quotations. "I am the sworn, eternal uncompromising enemy of the liquor traffic," he yelled. "I will fight the Wets 'till hell freezes over and then I'll buy a pair of skates and fight 'em on the ice."

Through an effective combination of talk and behind-the-scenes organization, Sunday converted an estimated 300,000 people to the temperance cause. Meetings in big cities sometimes attracted upwards of 40,000 people—more than typically came to see the president.

The antidrink message gradually took hold across all levels of society. Citizens flocked to the cause. Politicians jumped on the fast-moving Dry bandwagon, and numerous Dry candidates were elected to Congress just before World War I. By 1912, ten states had gone Dry.

But holding back the Drys' momentum was the fact that no federal law prohibited the interstate transportation of alcohol. A Dry state could not block alcohol shipped from its Wet neighbors. Nor could a Dry state halt the sale of liquor from a Wet state in its original packaging. In 1913, bowing to the Drys, Congress narrowly passed the Webb-Kenyon Act, which allowed Dry states to halt liquor deliveries at their borders.

The next year, Dry representatives attempted to pass a constitutional measure against alcohol. The law would have prohibited the manufacture and use of liquor in the United States. It failed . . . but just barely.

Backed by a flow of cash from antidrink forces, more Drys were sent to Washington after the 1916 congressional elections. The money came from the Anti-Saloon League and from multimillionaires such as variety store king Samuel Kresge and automaker Henry Ford. The Anti-Saloon League's combined plea of morality and spirituality found fertile ground with such well-heeled executives as Kresge and Ford. The corporate moguls figured that efficiency and profits would increase in their factories without alcohol and other vices to tempt their workers.

LIQUOR INDUSTRY FIGHTS BACK

With an estimated $2 billion a year in alcohol sales at stake, brewers didn't mind paying their association three cents per barrel to fight the Prohibition crowd. But the brewers and distillers made some tactical mistakes. They antagonized women, many of whom were lobbying for universal suffrage—the right to vote—as the Prohibition battle raged. During one convention, the brewers came out against suffrage, angering many women and pushing them into the Prohibition fight.

Women campaigning for suffrage also put their energy into the Prohibition effort.

"The fact that the brewers didn't care about us really made me mad," offered one Idaho woman. "So I went and joined our local temperance society." A housewife in upper New York state agreed: "By working hard to get the right to vote, I realized that I could make a difference. I then turned my attention to closing the saloons. We had so many in town."

The liquor industry printed tons of its own propaganda, much of it emphasizing the importance of the industry to jobs and the nation's economy. The tone of this material was just as angry as that of the Dry publications. In 1913, a magazine called *Barrels and Bottles* rapped the Anti-Saloon League as "the most arrogant organization of canting hypocrites . . . the world has ever seen."

As the Drys grew stronger, saloonkeepers fought to save their livelihoods.

While the Anti-Saloon League could call on churches and their congregations for help, the distillers and brewers had only the saloon keepers
to support them. In one issue of *Mixer and Server* magazine, a bartender
responded to the critics: "Running a saloon is purely a business proposi-
tion. Selling whiskey is less risky and more lucrative than many other
businesses. If I don't engage in it, someone else will."

Yet it was hard to defend a place called "the devil's headquarters on
earth." Billy Sunday, who always had something to say, leaped into the
debate:

> The saloon is the sum of all villainies. It is worse than war,
> worse than pestilence, worse than famine. It is the crime of
> crimes. It is the mother of sins. It is the appalling source of
> misery, pauperism and crime.

While many Protestant ministers echoed Sunday's message, most big-city Jewish and Catholic clergymen urged moderation rather than Prohibition. They argued that abstinence should be a matter of choice rather than law. But there was no organized anti-Prohibition group for those favoring a middle position. Individuals who opposed total abstinence had no place to turn for political action.

Meanwhile, the Drys grew more powerful. Large gifts of cash came from industrialists such as Henry Ford. Yet most donations came from middle-class and poor people. The average monthly pledge to the Anti-Saloon League was between 25 cents and two dollars. Between 1900 and 1919, the league received more than $2.5 million from such small donations. Firm in their beliefs, people willingly gave what little they had.

The tide was slowly turning away from the Wets. By 1917, 25 states were Dry—35 million citizens were affected. In January of that year, Congress outlawed liquor advertisements in Dry states. It also ordered Prohibition in the District of Columbia and the territories of Alaska, Puerto Rico, and Hawaii.

In Chicago, a newspaper humor columnist who wrote under the name of Mr. Dooley, penned a note to his pretend friend, Mr. Hennessey:

> I used to laugh at th' pro-hybitionists. I used to laugh them to scorn. But I laugh no more; they've got us on th' run . . . Whether ye like it or not, in a few years there won't be anny saloons to lure the marri'd man fr'm his home, furnish guests for our gr-reat asylums an' jails an' brighten up th' dark sthreets with their cheerful glow.

A bartender in West Virginia, worried that Prohibition might spread, warned his tobacco-spitting patrons: "Don't be alarmed if you soon spit talcum powder."

VICTORY AT HOME

With increasing financial and political strength, the Drys figured the time was right to make another move. They marshaled their supporters and eagerly charged into Washington for a big push. But they hadn't counted on global events temporarily derailing their cause. World War I wrenched the nation's attention away from the Prohibition debate. On April 6, 1917, the United States declared war on Germany.

Most of the nation was focused on the war in Europe. But the Drys never rested on the home battlefront. They argued that alcohol impaired military efficiency. Crops should be used to feed troops and allies in Europe, they said, not to make liquor. Congress passed the Food Control Bill and several other measures designed to conserve food for the war effort. These laws also effectively limited the amount of grain sold to breweries and distilleries.

Meanwhile, an anti-German hysteria was sweeping the nation. In a reactionary frenzy, sauerkraut was renamed "liberty cabbage" and such old-line institutions as the staid Deutcher (German) Club in Milwaukee became the Wisconsin Club. Many prominent American brewers were of

—By courtesy of the Farm Journal.

Where Is Your Corn Going, Neighbor?

A bushel of corn makes four gallons of whiskey, which retails at	$16.70
The farmer gets	.50
The railroad gets	.80
The distiller gets	4.00
The government gets	4.40
The saloonkeeper gets	7.00
The consumer gets	Drunk
The wife and children get	Nothing but rags and sorrow

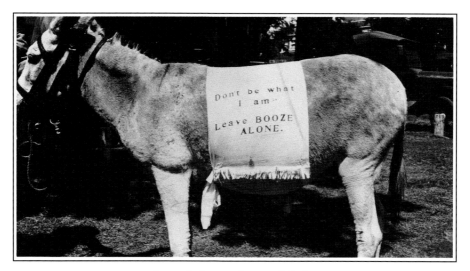

A special warning to drinkers

German heritage; even the manufacture of beer was considered "too German." The falloff in alcohol production was considered truly patriotic.

The Drys remained busy, raising the idea of a constitutional amendment again and again. The demands for Prohibition were especially strong from rural states in the West and Deep South. Few states with major cities favored restrictions on drinking. But in June 1917, a Senate committee met to discuss an amendment that would outlaw the production and sale of liquor in the United States. Two months later, 65 senators voted in favor of the amendment. Only 20 voted nay.

What helped the measure pass was a clause saying that the law would not go into effect unless three-quarters of the states (36) ratified it within six years. A compromise amendment added another year, for a total of seven. Wet senators figured that no Prohibition legislation would pass in that amount of time. So they celebrated, even though the vote went against them.

The measure was presented to the House of Representatives late in 1917. Just before Christmas, wild debate raged over the pros and cons of such a law. The full force of the powerful Anti-Saloon League was called into play. Drys sent hundreds of telegrams and letters—many under made-up names—to increase the pressure on Congress. Posters placed in churches and businesses urged: "Close the Saloons. If you believe that the traffic in alcohol does more harm than good—Help Stop It!" A drawing accompanying the words showed a woman with a sledge hammer about to smash a bottle, while two bartenders cowered in the corner.

Overwhelmed, representative after representative joined the Dry forces. When the vote came to the House floor on December 18, it passed 282 to 128. Still, the Wets never thought that 36 state legislatures would support the measure within the seven-year limit.

But they were taken totally by surprise. Eager Drys controlled many state legislatures. The Anti-Saloon League called in all its political debts and charged out in support of the cause. The first state to cast the "yes" vote was Mississippi. State after state followed, caught up in a barrage of Dry propaganda.

Meanwhile, as the states voted, drinkers stocked up on private reserves. They hid whiskey in warehouses, basements, and barns. Bottles were secreted away in safe-deposit boxes.

Liquor dealers urged drinkers to stock up as the start of national Prohibition drew near.

But there was no stopping the Dry tide. Within one year and eight days, 36 states had voted in favor of the Eighteenth Amendment. Nebraska cast the deciding vote on January 16, 1919. Ten more states followed. Only Connecticut and Rhode Island stood firmly opposed to the amendment. Prohibition would go into effect at midnight on Saturday, January 17, 1920.

As passed, the Eighteenth Amendment outlawed the manufacture, sale, transportation, import, and export of intoxicating liquor in the United States. It also gave Congress and the states power to enforce the amendment. Rules of enforcement were spelled out in the National Prohibition Act, or Volstead Act, named after Congressman Andrew Volstead of Minnesota. (Volstead chaired the House Judiciary Committee that prepared the final draft of the act. But the law was actually drawn up by Wayne Wheeler, national attorney for the Anti-Saloon League and one of the most powerful behind-the-scenes figures in American politics at the time.)

For a brief moment, Prohibition stalled. On October 27, 1919, President Woodrow Wilson vetoed the Volstead Act. Congress had linked Prohibition to wartime grain conservation. But World War I was over. Grain conservation was no longer needed, Wilson argued. The veto made no difference. Eager legislators overrode Wilson on October 28.

William H. Anderson, head of the New York Anti-Saloon League, told the Wets to be good sports when the amendment received its final approval. "Shake hands with Uncle Sam," he said.

DRY DAY AT LAST

It was a cold, wet night in January when the final bell tolled at midnight for drinkers. Mock funerals were held for "John Barleycorn" (alcohol personified) with coffins paraded through the streets. Billy Sunday led 10,000 "mourners" in a funeral service in Norfolk, Virginia. "Goodbye, John," Sunday said. "You were God's worst enemy; you were hell's best friend. I hate you with a perfect hatred. I love to hate you."

Newspapers told about raucous parties held in those final hours on the last day of legal drinking. But in many places, the mood was somber.

In Detroit, rain put a stop to outdoor celebrations. An anticipated riot of angry drinkers did not occur. The streets were almost deserted, and hundreds of mounted police officers were sent home early. At a party in the Park Avenue Hotel in Philadelphia, black cloth covered the walls, guests and servers wore black, and the last drinks were served in black glasses. In the center of the dance floor sat a coffin filled with empty bottles. In cities around the country, buglers polished up their instruments and sounded a mournful taps for liquor. On street corners, people sang a new musical hit, "The Alcohol Blues."

While Prohibition would last 14 years, America stayed Dry less than a day. In fact, the lawlessness kicked in almost immediately. At 12:01 A.M., on January 17, 1920, six gunmen burst into a shed in a Chicago railroad yard, tied up the guard, and made off with two freight cars full of alcohol valued at $100,000. Shortly afterward, across town, four barrels of

Wayne Wheeler

Andrew Volstead

A last legal drink, January 16, 1920

grain alcohol were stolen from a government warehouse. In a third incident in the predawn hours of that first official Dry day, a gang hijacked a truck full of whiskey that had just been stolen from another site. Already, the gangsters were feeding on each other.

But the forces of law were already at work as well. In New York, agents raided a Chinese restaurant and smashed bottles of whiskey. Three hundred saloon keepers in Camden, New Jersey, were caught selling whiskey, and well-armed federal agents headed to Michigan's Upper Peninsula to smash a stash of hidden wine barrels found near Iron River.

The battle lines had been drawn.

SCOFFLAWS AND SMUGGLERS

Take three ounces every hour for stimulant until stimulated.

—Doctor's prescription
for medicinal alcohol

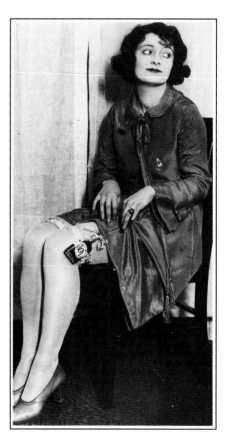

Under the Volstead Act, people could drink liquor that they had acquired before Prohibition, provided it was consumed in their own homes. Drinkers could manufacture "nonintoxicating" (defined as having less than .5 percent alcohol) cider and fruit juice, again at home. The law also allowed the manufacture and sale (by those with special permits) of alcohol for medicinal, industrial, and religious uses. All other alcohol was illegal.

A reluctant Bureau of Internal Revenue was given the responsibility of seeing that the demands of the Eighteenth Amendment and the Volstead Act were followed to the letter. About 1,500 poorly paid federal agents were hired, given little training, and sent out to enforce the law of the land. Prohibitionists were so confident in their cause that they never figured enforcing the amendment would be a problem.

But for those who would turn a blind eye to the law, the United States was perfect. It had 12,000 miles of coastline, 3,700 miles of land borders, and 3,000 miles along the Great Lakes and connecting rivers, all of which could be penetrated by smugglers. Plugging the breach would be an impossible task. Law enforcement agencies were underfunded and the court system overworked. Frequently, police and government officials could be bribed. And the American people—many of whom still wanted to drink—were generally indifferent as to whether or not the new regulations were enforced.

For many Americans, in fact, the advent of Prohibition seemed like an invitation to hold an open party. Now that the United States had the law it supposedly wanted, there was almost a secret glee in seeing how much could be gotten away with, despite the penalties.

BATHTUB GIN AND POP MOON

One way to get alcohol was to make it. That was usually the job of the "bootlegger," a name for someone who made, smuggled, or sold illegal liquor. The nickname came from frontier days in Oklahoma Territory, when smugglers carried flasks of illegal whiskey tucked inside their high boots.

But home-cooked drink could be deadly, distilled as it often was from wood or industrial alcohol. One beverage labeled bourbon was actually made from iodine and burned sugar. Another was a vile mixture of prune juice, caramel coloring, and creosote, an oil-based pitch used to keep telephone and fence poles from rotting. The famous Prohibition-era "bathtub gin" was made from juniper oil, glycerin, and other hard-to-swallow ingredients. Some people believed that wood alcohol was safe to drink if it had been filtered through a slice of bread. It's no wonder that many people died from drinking Pop Moon, Yack Yack, and Jake— names given to some of the nastier concoctions.

Stills were everywhere, hidden in the mist-shrouded hills of Kentucky and secreted in hot city attics and musty basements. The notorious Genna brothers ran Chicago's Little Italy like their own distillery. They hired hundreds of immigrant families as "alky cookers," producing cheap whiskey in home stills. The Gennas provided the materials and the protection. No one said "no" to the brothers, who had a list of murders to their credit that ran several pages. Besides, the locals always appreciated the few extra dollars that their stills provided to the family coffers.

Production of homemade wine also soared. Under the new law, heads of households were allowed to make up to 200 gallons of fermented "fruit juice" per year, if they had the proper permit. Between 1920 and 1930, production of homemade wine topped the 100 million gallon mark. Assuredly, all that vintage was not consumed by private households. Much of it probably found its way onto the illegal market.

A do-it-yourself distillery in Kentucky

There was much humor in home-based operations, as pointed out by Ethan Mordden in his book *All That Jazz!* Mordden quotes noted journalist H. L. Mencken: "Last Sunday, I manufactured five gallons of 'Methodistbrau.' But I bottled it too soon and the result has been a series of fearful explosions." Two of his jugs blew up, bringing Mencken's neighbor out of his house, thinking "the Soviets had seized the town."

The most popular way to carry illicit alcohol about the streets, right under the nose of the authorities, was with a hip flask, a thin container that fit into a back pocket. Other devices were used: baby carriages with false bottoms, hollowed-out books, and empty coconuts. Women concealed bottles in their corsets and garter belts. One well-known singer kept her stash hidden in a piano. Sometimes even schoolkids delivered booze in backpacks or lunch buckets. On one occasion, a harmonica-playing elephant got rambunctious after a vaudeville performance in Milwaukee. The grumpy giant knocked down a wall of its stall. Hidden behind the shattered partition were several thousand bottles of prime whiskey, rum, vermouth, gin, and other hard-to-get liquors.

For all their talk about Prohibition, members of Congress also knew where to get a drink. One small room in the Capitol was reserved for the "Board of Education." Actually, it was a quiet place where the most powerful representatives and senators could retire for a chat and a drink. Bottles were hidden inside books on the shelves that lined the room. Whiskey-loving President Warren G. Harding was known to keep a bottle handy. One of the duties of the treasurer of the Republican National Committee was to make sure an ample supply of drink and cigars was on hand for the president's twice-a-week poker parties. Harding could have gotten his own whiskey easily enough: more than 500 bootleggers worked the neighborhoods within three blocks of the White House.

"THE LAWLESS DRINKER"

Some people lost their jobs because of the Eighteenth Amendment, a factor not initially considered by the Anti-Saloon League and its cohorts. Some saloon owners turned to running speakeasies—illegal nightclubs. Others continued operations legally, opening soda fountains or restaurants.

Breweries, now called "cereal beverage producers," had to content themselves with manufacturing "near beer"—containing less than .5 percent alcohol. Miller Brewing Company made a drink named High Life. Schlitz developed Schlitz-flavored Malt Syrup. Both products skated close to the alcohol limit, but were legal. Some breweries were converted into factories that made soda pop, chocolate candy, malt, chewing gum, or cheese. Yet the restrictions drove other firms, such as Anheuser-Busch, almost out of business.

More than a few ex-brewers drifted outside the law. Their skills were valuable to gangsters operating illegal plants. The crooks bought off the cops and politicians, while the beer makers did what they did best. Gambrinius, Pfeffer, Stege, and Phenix were among the quality beers secretly produced in the traditional way. They were distributed by such toughs as Owney (the Killer) Madden, Frankie Lake, Johnny Torrio, and others whose reputations were enhanced by a history of prison terms.

But even normally law-abiding citizens became "scofflaws," a term used to denote anyone who ignored Prohibition laws. The word was submitted for a contest devised in 1923 by a rich prohibitionist from Quincy, Massachusetts. Two winners split $200 for their creative efforts, but the competition failed to convince "the lawless drinker to stab awake his conscience" as intended.

Typical of the ordinary people who broke the law was Minnie Elder of Milwaukee, a widowed scrubwoman at the Cream City Brewery. The brewery now made near beer—and plenty of "real stuff" on the side. Each Sunday, Elder rode the streetcar to her relatives' home. In her shopping bag, she always carried a gallon jug of beer, given to her by the *bräumeister,* the head brew master.

One day, there was a loud bang on the streetcar. Everyone turned to look at the frail old lady and her black bag. The cork in Elder's jug had exploded, and beer spewed all over the seats. The people on the trolley had a good laugh, and nobody turned Elder over to the police. Although she was embarrassed by the incident, she kept delivering beer to her relatives each week—even though one of her daughters was married to a police officer, a strong supporter of Prohibition.

Agents find booze hidden in a truckload of lumber.

For years, the Elder family kept a recipe for home brew, provided to Minnie by the bräumeister. Typed on official Cream City Brewery stationery, the recipe gave step-by-step instructions for combining hops, sugar, malt extract, water, and yeast. The most critical step, fermentation for 60 to 70 days, turned the mixture into beer. In the last sentence of the recipe the bräumeister warned: "Omit fermentation in dry territory."

Those who didn't care to try their hand at home brewing had other options. The law allowed the use of liquor for "medicinal purposes," a term that took on broad meaning during Prohibition. One doctor in Highland Park, Michigan, treated hundreds of workers from the nearby Chrysler plant. The patients complained of "shaky nerves." The prescribed treatment? A pint of high-grade whiskey. The nearest drugstore, one floor below the doctor's office, filled prescriptions pint by pint. The arrangement was legal—sort of—and both doctor and druggist made money.

But there were dangers, even with drinking at home. While the police didn't usually bother with scofflaws, Dry employers often did. Ford Motor Company payed a generous wage—five dollars for an eight-hour workday. But auto workers paid a price in return. Insisting that workers conform to certain moral standards, Henry Ford started a "sociology department." His agents visited workers in their homes and offered tips on health, cleanliness, and nutrition. The agents also checked to see whether workers were drinking. Drinking at home, although not technically illegal, was grounds for dismissal. Ford wasn't alone. The REO Motor Car Company and others in Detroit were just as strict.

THE COAST IS CLEAR

Most illegal liquor came from America's Wet neighbors. Canada imported six times as much liquor as it had prior to Prohibition; most of this alcohol was then smuggled into the United States. It was the same with other countries near the border: Mexican imports rose eight times; West Indian, five times. The Department of Commerce estimated that by early 1922, two years after the Eighteenth Amendment went into effect, more than $40 million worth of liquor had been sneaked into the states.

Profits soared, with smugglers selling their illegal loads for three to four times what they paid for them. Sometimes, the good stuff was diluted with water or other liquid to make it go further. When someone said he had "the real McCoy," that meant quality, uncut whiskey. The term came from William (Big Bill) McCoy, a smuggler who operated out of Nassau, the Bahamas.

McCoy bragged that he carried only the best contraband aboard his swift schooner, the *Tomoka*. Eventually captured, he was convicted under the Volstead Act and sent to Atlanta's federal penitentiary in 1925. He was cheeky to the end. After his arrest at sea, McCoy supposedly threatened to hijack the Coast Guard cutter bringing him to shore, saying he'd use it in his rum-running trade.

Called "mother ships," oceangoing freighters carrying liquor anchored just three miles offshore. Under international law, the police and Coast Guard could not go beyond that watery boundary in pursuit of alcohol.

Coast Guard cutter on patrol

To avoid arrest, a rumrunner dumps his cargo, destroying the evidence against him.

Unloading confiscated whiskey at a New York pier, July 1924

So the smugglers thumbed their noses at the law, riding on the lazy ocean swells just out of reach. Then, under cover of night, swift speedboats picked up the illegal cargo and delivered it to coves and harbors from Maine to Florida, throughout the Gulf of Mexico, and along the West Coast. From there, the cargo was sent inland. The rumrunners, or "rummies," were aided by hidden onshore radio stations, which beamed the location of prowling Coast Guard cutters. Operators called out "the coast is clear" when danger was past.

In response, the authorities outfitted a flotilla of vessels, including 20 sleek destroyers that had plowed the seas in World War I. Yet even these tough veterans of many naval battles, staffed by handpicked crews, had a hard time keeping up with the tiny speedboats—the "pullers"—that scooted across the water like bugs.

If warned, smugglers could easily evade capture. If luck wasn't with them, just before they were caught, rumrunners would simply dump their cargo overboard. Without evidence, no charges could be issued. Sometimes, abandoned contraband was weighted down with salt. When the salt later dissolved, it released a buoy that led smugglers back to the liquor hidden beneath the blue-green waves.

Hard-pressed, stressed, and ill paid, the authorities were always on the run. On their limited government budgets, they were usually a step behind the gangsters.

CANADIAN CLUB

Smuggling alcohol into border cities like Detroit was easy. The Detroit River separating Canada from the United States is barely a mile wide. With a ready supply of drink on one side and a thirsty clientele on the other, rumrunners got their goods across the border in double-quick time. Once loaded into trucks waiting on the Detroit docks, the liquor disappeared within minutes. While automaker Henry Ford was an ardent prohibitionist, it is interesting to note that his dependable Model T car was used by both big and small smugglers to haul their wares. Many rumrunners owed their success to the old "flivvers," as the cars were nicknamed.

Rum-running didn't guarantee a long life. Far from it. We'll never know how many smugglers were killed hitting reefs in the fog and darkness or were murdered by hijackers. Yet there was no shortage of those willing to go after a fast buck, despite the hardships, fear, and danger.

But it was necessary to think really big to make really big money. Although it was illegal to make, sell, or ship alcohol within the United States, it was still legal to ship alcohol between Canada and Mexico, across the United States. Diverting loaded freight cars—right into smugglers' hands—was simple. But to succeed, it was necessary to have a combination of organization, street smarts, luck, money . . . and machine guns.

THE DARK UNDERSIDE

All I ever did was supply a demand that was pretty popular . . . . All I ever did was to sell beer and whiskey to our best people . . . . Why, some of the leading judges use the stuff. . . . If people did not want beer and wouldn't drink it, a fellow would be crazy for going around trying to sell it.

—Al Capone

Money, money, money. The demand for drink created a ready and willing market, and every gangster wanted a major piece of the action. That desire led to bloody, gun-chattering rivalries, as territories were fought over like medieval fiefdoms and greed spread into all walks of life.

At least at first, rumrunners and mobsters were looked upon as serving a need. The public sometimes even helped criminals escape the police—because the gangsters were seen as Robin Hoods, helping out the little guy. But the lawlessness quickly got out of hand. In Detroit, some schools had to keep children inside during recess because gangster shootouts made neighborhoods too dangerous. So many mobsters were shot to death on one intersection in Cleveland that it was called Bloody Corner.

Colorful but vicious warlords—Frank Costello in New York City, Philadelphia's Maxie Hoff, Chicago's "Scarface" Al Capone and Dion O'Banion, Chester LeMare in Kansas City—ruled criminal empires. Around the edges were the freelancers, killers and rumrunners such as Murder, Inc., the Purple Gang, Legs Diamond, and a host of comparable thugs and thieves. The gang leaders considered themselves so powerful that the always-quotable Arthur (Dutch Schultz) Flegenheimer supposedly once said he gave the New York police department 24 hours to get out of town.

STREETS OF GOLD

From the end of the 19th century through the early 1920s, millions of immigrants flocked to the United States from all corners of the world. Bringing their dreams, muscle, creativity, and talent, they were ready to do whatever was necessary to prosper in a land where streets supposedly

A violin case makes a clever container for a sawed-off shotgun.

were paved with gold. Most immigrants settled in and worked hard at legitimate jobs. But others put their skills to work in a different direction.

For some young immigrants, crime was the fastest way to potential fame and riches. Clustering in neighborhood and ethnic groups, some immigrants formed street gangs. They allied themselves with whomever offered the best deals, or they carved out their own kingdoms. But while family and ethnic ties were important, it made no difference if a mobster's mother tongue was Yiddish, German, Italian, English, Gaelic, or Polish. Everyone understood the word for money.

Of course, there were dangers. The wrong word, the lack of a payoff, or a deal gone bad could all lead to a "ride in the country" or a "swim in concrete overshoes." Either way, death was the usual outcome. The first person known to be taken for such a one-way journey during the era was small-time gangster Giuseppe Nazarro, alias Joe Chuck, whose bullet-riddled corpse was found alongside the railroad tracks in Yonkers, New York, in 1919.

Frankie Uale, boss of the Italian gangs in Brooklyn, took a car ride one evening in 1927. Unfortunately for him, he rolled down his bulletproof windows to enjoy the warm breeze. That was a fatal mistake. Dozens of .45-caliber slugs racked the limousine and quickly ended Uale's climb up the criminal career-ladder. Nobody admitted to the killing, but his buddies put Uale away in real style. He was laid out in a $15,000 silver casket, holding a solid gold rosary. The funeral cortege, the procession to the cemetery, stretched five miles. More than $37,000 in floral arrangements overflowed the mortuary and the grave site. One wreath marked the time of Uale's death in violets, with a streamer that read, "We'll get 'em, kid." That message was not hard to interpret.

Among the worst offenders were members of the Mafia, brought to the United States from Sicily, Italy, in 1899. At first, the Mafia was only one of numerous groups vying for control of the lucrative liquor trade and associated criminal activity ranging from prostitution to loan sharking to gambling. Because of their ruthlessness, Mafia leaders gradually gained more power than the other mobsters. Sawed-off shotguns, .38 revolvers, knives, bombs, and Thompson submachine guns (nicknamed "tommy guns," "choppers," and "Chicago pianos") were in their arsenals as they fought each other and anyone else who stood in their way.

TOP MOBSTER

Alphonse Caponi—Al Capone—an Italian-born New York tough guy, eventually became the biggest name in the mobster business. Capone went to Chicago in 1919, handpicked by Johnny Torrio to help run a gang. Torrio used a lethal combination of muscle and street smarts to weave numerous small Chicago gangs into a large umbrella group. As Torrio's lieutenant, Capone learned his lessons well.

Witness what happened to Spike O'Donnell shortly after he was released from jail. The Irish mobster and his three brothers immediately ran into stiff bootlegging competition from Torrio and his sidekick, Capone. Within a year, O'Donnell had been attacked at least ten times by Torrio's gang. Seven of O'Donnell's men, including his brother Walter, were murdered. The heat was enough to send Spike fleeing the state.

Spike O'Donnell, 1930

Capone ruled a gangster empire.

Capone's scarred face, earned as a young man in a fight with a razor-wielding opponent, became a symbol of his viciousness. In October 1925, Torrio returned to Italy, fleeing a growing army of enemies. Capone stepped in, placing his own allies in top mob positions. But three rivals plotted against Scarface Al, who soon found out about their secret dealings through informers. He invited the conspirators to dinner at the Burnham Hotel one evening and, after dessert, told them he knew of their plans. He then used a baseball bat to beat to death the panic-stricken guests of honor. The message didn't take long to make the rounds: Capone was in charge. Nobody, but nobody, messed with him.

At the height of his power, the dapper killer had some 700 mobsters in his private army and made more than sixty million untaxed dollars a year. "Everybody calls me a racketeer. I call myself a businessman," he once said. "When my patrons serve my booze on a silver tray on Lake [Shore] Drive, it's hospitality."

ART IMITATES LIFE

Americans were intrigued. Despite the bloodshed, gangsters captured the public's imagination—especially from the safety of a movie house. There were some 21,000 movie theaters in the United States by 1925, each running more than 700 shows a year. The movie moguls were in business to make money. And gangster movies made loads of money.

Underworld, written by Ben Hecht in 1927, was one of the first popular gangster flicks. The story describes a love triangle between bank robber Bull Weed (played by George Bancroft), his girlfriend Feathers McCoy (Evelyn Brent), and drunken lawyer Rolls Royce (Clive Brook). Feathers falls in love with Rolls when he gives up drinking, and Bull becomes furious. The result is plenty of gunfire, flashing headlights, and racing cars.

From then on, gangster films were full of action. Always guaranteeing a full house were gritty productions like *Little Caesar* (1930), *Public Enemy* (1931), and *Scarface* (1932). "Tough guy" character actors launched distinguished careers in such films. Whenever Paul Muni, Edward G. Robinson, George Raft, or James Cagney strolled across the towering screens in the ornate movie palaces of the era, viewers were assured of a spine-tingling show.

The stars' sneers and smart-aleck back talk struck fear—and probably admiration—in the hearts of a generation of young theatergoers. The bad guys dressed well, had fancy autos, and had the best-looking molls, or girlfriends, on their arms—even if they did meet an unhealthy end in the gutter. When Eddie Barlett is shot down in *The Roaring Twenties,* his girlfriend, Panama Smith, holds him in her arms. "He used to be a big shot," she says. Audiences cried. Mae West became a legend for her spoofs of the classic dame out to make a buck with the bad guys. Of one of her characters West remarked, "She climbed the ladder of success, wrong by wrong."

Authenticity was very important. Director Lewis Milestone hired eight Chicago bootleggers who were hiding out in Los Angeles as advisers for *The Racket* (1928). The gangsters did their job well: some people thought the film was *too* authentic. Milestone's piece depicted a corrupt mayor in action and demonstrated the tight relationship between criminals and politicians. The New York Motion Picture Commission demanded that

Paul Muni in **Scarface**

scenes of criminals bribing police officers be edited out. *The Racket* was banned in Chicago when the mayor there, Big Bill Thompson (who was fairly close with the mobsters himself), complained.

In an attempt to protect themselves from outsiders and to disguise their intentions from police, gangsters developed highly colorful slang that eventually made its way into mainstream American speech. The following telephone conversation between two mobsters is typical, as related by researchers Gordon L. Hostetter and Thomas Quinn Beesley in a report on hoodlum language in 1929:

> A squad o' dicks in monkey suits wuz rifflin de wops' joint on a squawk from some clunk who'd been took for a couple o' fins dere wit' some tops. While they wuz casin' it, a runner drove up to de family entrance wit' a load o' merchandise and the apron had a tough job slippin' im de office not to unload. He wuz afraid the flatties would want a split and the damper didn't have enough grease for a nix crack.

Translated, the conversation went:

> A detail of plainclothes detectives was searching the Italians' saloon without a warrant after a complaint from some fool who'd been cheated of ten dollars there with some loaded dice. While they were searching the premises, a smuggler drove up to the secret entrance with a load of alcohol and the bartender had a tough job giving him the signal not to unload. He was afraid the plainclothesmen would expect a share and there wasn't enough cash in the drawer to buy their silence.

Scriptwriters, novelists, and journalists loved such punchy new words that added pizzazz to their own writing. "On the lam," "stool pigeon," "bump off," "big shot," and thousands of other phrases became popular.

And through it all, people kept on drinking—except when they were ducking bullets.

ROARING TWENTIES

The Cotton Club, Hoofer's, Ciro's, Connie's Inn, Club Durant. These were the speakeasies—illegal nightclubs. Exclusive, secretive, and romantic, the speakeasy was like a sealed honey pot in an anthill: the harder it was to gain access, the more people wanted in.

According to H. L. Mencken, the term "speakeasy" might have evolved from the Irish "speak softly shop," designating an unlicensed public house, or pub. Inside, it was necessary to "speak easy" to avoid going to jail . . . or worse. Whatever its origin, the speakeasy became a symbol of the Eighteenth Amendment's ineffectiveness.

When one thinks of the 1920s—nicknamed the "Roaring Twenties" and the "Jazz Age"—the speakeasy often comes to mind. The highly visible saloons of older days were easy targets for the antidrink crowd. But speakeasies were secret clubs, often tucked into basements, attics, and the back ends of warehouses. They were difficult to find for good reason. No one wanted the "wrong crowd," namely the police, to burst in and break the bubble of fun.

Secrecy added to the speakeasy's thrill. The front of a speakeasy might look like a simple barbershop, a somber funeral parlor, or an ordinary grocery store. But behind the false fronts were sliding doors and hidden panels leading to barrooms. To gain entrance to the darkly mysterious— but always exciting—interior universe, customers had to give passwords. "Joe sent me" was a common greeting.

While most speakeasies were small, crowded, and dirty, others were elaborate. Famous performers—comedian Jimmy Durante, singer Cab Calloway, and musician Duke Ellington—launched their careers from these clubs. Patrons flocked to the most prestigious speakeasies to see shows. One famous hideaway, hidden behind a bowling alley, came complete with a 100-foot-long bar and 20 bartenders.

Within two years of Prohibition's enactment, an estimated 32,000 to 100,000 speakeasies were operating in New York City alone. "All you need is a bottle and two glasses to open a place," snorted one tired police officer. Many famous cocktails got their start during these days. The Manhattan, originally made with rye whiskey, vermouth, bitters, and a slice of lemon, was first mixed in a speakeasy. Nonalcoholic ingredients were often needed to mask the foul flavor of cut-rate alcohol.

Two flamboyant women vied for the title "Queen of the Speakeasies." Both worked the New York scene and were the subjects of numerous newspaper stories. One candidate was Belle Livingston. She operated a five-story bar, complete with a miniature golf course and Ping-Pong tables. Admission to her plush Country Club, located on trendy East Fifty-eighth Street, was a mere five dollars. But drinks soared up to $40 for a bottle of champagne.

Livingston's biggest rival for the crown was Mary Louise (Texas) Guinan, whose flashy trademark was a bracelet made with 600 diamonds. The former bronc rider from Waco, Texas, was also noted for her gravel-voiced greeting: "Hello, Sucker." Guinan's speakeasy, Texas'

Liquor was plentiful in this speakeasy but chairs were not. So customers sat on wooden packing crates.

El Fay Club on West Forty-fifth Street, was fronted by mobster Larry Fay. The club was raided so often that every time a federal agent stood up to make his arrests, the band would immediately start playing "The Prisoner's Song."

"CHARLESTON, CHARLESTON!"

The speakeasy opened the door to a different world, one that shattered old-time barriers in morals and manners. With new inventions and the growth of big cities, it seemed natural for Americans to break from the restrictions of a more conservative past. The speakeasy was the place where that could happen.

Americans of a generation earlier would never have imagined that women would smoke and drink in public, that teenagers would neck in the backseats of cars and in darkened theater balconies, or that young women would roll their stockings beneath the knee. These were startling developments in an era when many older women still wore corsets— tight-fitting undergarments fastened by laces.

Imitating romantic stars of the silent screen, young women rushed to "bob" their hair. Mary C. Detmers of Whittier, California, recalls:

> The year was 1924 and I was 14 years old. I'd just pleaded with Mother for permission to have my hair bobbed and again she said no. My 16-year-old sister, Alice, and I were the only girls in our school who still had long hair. When popular movie stars like Gloria Swanson and Colleen Moore had bobbed their hair, many girls and women followed. But some, like Mother, saw bobbed hair as immoral.

Within a year, though, even Detmers' old-fashioned mother had bobbed her hair. America was changing.

The new generation with its "flappers"—leggy young women in sequined mini-dresses and long beaded necklaces—loved wild dances like the Charleston and the Lindy. The sensuous tango, with its long, sliding steps, appeared from Latin America and offered sultry mystery to a decade seemingly gone crazy in the pursuit of fun.

Movie star Clara Bow, the "It Girl," became the symbol of the younger generation's flashy new lifestyle. Coined by author Elinor Glyn, the term "it" meant "cool." If kids didn't have that hard-to-define it factor, they feared they'd be left out of the fun. F. Scott Fitzgerald's novels *This Side of Paradise* (1920) and *The Great Gatsby* (1925) are famous for their portrayals of the glamorous it lifestyle, in which fast cars, loads of money, and snappy clothes meant everything, even if the stories ended tragically.

Young people curled up with magazines such as *True Romances* and *True Lovers* and racy novels like *Unforbidden Fruit*. Students repeated jokes from *College Humor* magazine:

> First Flapper: The boy I'm going out with now thinks of nothing but necking.
>
> Second Flapper: What can you do with a fellow like that?
>
> First Flapper: Neck.

Needless to say, such lines were not received well by most mothers and fathers.

It seemed as if the older and younger generations spoke different languages. "We'd say, 'Oh you, kid' and 'the cat's pajamas' whenever we thought something was really exciting," laughed one Iowan, recalling her teenage years in the 1920s. "Our parents couldn't figure out what we were talking about." Songs echoed the tone of the times. "The Best Things in Life Are Free," claimed one tune. "Yes, We Have No Bananas" was another silly ditty repeated over and over, much to the dismay of adults who had to listen.

The movies offered their share of excitement. Dark-eyed heartthrob Rudolph Valentino made his film debut in 1919 in *The Eyes of Youth*. Advertisements billed his character as "Clarence Morgan, a cabaret parasite." Women went wild over Valentino's sexy looks and fluttering eyelashes, just as men went crazy over the heart-shaped face of Clara Bow and the curves of Gloria Swanson. The stars did things on the screen that would have been unthinkable only a few years earlier. From racy films such as *Married Flirts*—ads for the movie asked if wives knew where their husbands were—it was a short leap to real-life sex, gambling, drinking, and drug scandals among the Hollywood crowd. Both on screen and off, a new morality was sweeping the nation.

But not every film embraced the trend. The tearful *Face on the Barroom Floor* (1923) echoed the familiar Dry message. The film tells of a family that falls apart when Father becomes a drunkard.

"BEWARE OF BOOZE SHEIKS"

Alarmed parents warned their daughters to keep away from "booze sheiks"—rakish dandies in canary yellow and blazing red roadsters. The "sheik," with his pencil-thin mustache and slicked-back hair, would always have a flask of whiskey with him and a smooth song for the girls.

Dancing the Charleston. Even South Carolina Congressman T. S. McMillen—he's from Charleston—gets in on the fun.

Gloria Swanson in Male and Female. *With their sexy stars and steamy plotlines, silent movies were almost scandalous.*

And while very few women would have been seen in an old-time barroom, women were always welcome in the speakeasy. Young women popped into the secret nightclubs with or without male escorts. This behavior was unheard of in earlier decades, when "ladies" seldom went anywhere on their own.

Visiting a speakeasy was often dangerous. But, "Who cared?" remarked one woman, thinking back on her twenties. "After all, this was liberation. We felt free to do anything we wanted. Nobody could tell us what to do."

And where the girls were, the boys usually followed. So speakeasy owners were always assured of a crowd. Ironically, the very vices that prohibitionists frowned on—drinking, dancing, sex, and big-city life—grew even more common with the passage of the Eighteenth Amendment. Drinking seemed more exciting than ever after it became illegal.

The temperance tale **Ten Nights in a Barroom** *was written in 1855 and made into a movie in 1929. In this scene, Little Mary begs her father to come home from the Sickle and Sheaf tavern.*

Alert officials tried their best to put a stop to the law-breaking. In 1923, Sacramento Police Chief Bernard McShane wrote:

> Investigation substantiates the numerous complaints I have received that young girls are being supplied with liquor at dances and other social affairs in Sacramento. This is a most serious situation when one considers what might result from such practices.

That same year, the *San Francisco Examiner* reported:

> Pitiless publicity will be resorted to by Sheriff George A. Walters to stamp out wild drinking parties staged by boys and girls of high school age at roadhouses near Detroit. Fatherly advice having met with a toss of pretty bobbed head, the sheriff announces that all persons caught in liquor raids will be subpoenaed to testify against proprietors of such places, where, he charges, shocking conditions exist.

Dance crazy in St. Louis

But whatever the police did—whether raiding dances or breaking up roadhouse parties—was never enough. The drinking went on.

The 1920s were a time of change in the United States—change from a slow-paced agricultural society to a more hectic world. Thousands of folks moved from farms to cities to find work. Women entered the labor force in large numbers—working as sewing machine operators, sales clerks, teachers, waitresses, secretaries, and maids. In 1920, women won the right to vote. The Model T cost only $290. Cars gave people more mobility. And other new inventions, such as radio, provided immediate information. The 1920 presidential election was the first in history to be covered by radio reporters.

With lifestyle changes, advances in technology, and the ability to move around the country, young people could see a limitless future. Nobody was going to hold them back. Nobody. Not even the government and its Prohibition laws.

YOU'RE PINCHED!

This law will be obeyed in cities large and small, and in villages, and where it is not obeyed, it will be enforced. The law says that liquor to be used as a beverage must not be manufactured. We shall see that it is not manufactured. Not sold, not given away, not hauled in anything on the surface of the earth or under the earth or in the air.

—John F. Kramer,
Prohibition Commissioner

Enforcing Prohibition was no easy job. With law-breaking widespread and government resources in short supply, often it was only luck that brought bootleg liquor to the attention of the police. Many mobsters had community leaders in their back pockets. Worse yet, between 1927 and 1930, corrupt officials in Pottawatomie County, Oklahoma, actually controlled the area's liquor trade. A grand jury eventually brought more than 100 officials to justice, including the county attorney and a former sheriff.

Law-abiding officials, meanwhile, received little support. Oklahoma judge Robert L. Williams lamented that "a candidate for sheriff could not possibly be elected" if it was known he meant to enforce Prohibition. One police officer in Tonkawa, Oklahoma, was fired after he gave federal agents information about area bootleggers.

Even when a gangster was arrested, he was often out on the street immediately. Spike O'Donnell was sentenced to serve a term for bank robbery in 1923. But the governor of Illinois received a petition asking for

O'Donnell's release. Hundreds of leading citizens—including five state representatives, six senators, and a judge—had signed it. O'Donnell was pardoned. He went back to the Windy City to reestablish himself as one of the city's prime bootleggers—for a time.

General Smedley D. Butler, a World War I hero, was brought to Philadelphia by the mayor to help clean up the city's crime problem. As head of public safety, the hardworking Butler and his men made 2,000 arrests during his first week on the job. But cops and judges released the offenders as fast as Butler brought them in. Within a year, the frustrated and angry general went back to the marines, where life seemed easier.

"ETHICS BE HANGED"

A few Prohibition agents were little more than shakedown artists, always holding out their hands for a payoff in exchange for leaving a joint alone. Police officers were often guaranteed free drinks and meals when they

A raid on the Stork Club, 1932. Agents confiscated everything, even the chairs and tables.

FEDERAL
OFFICER

The
BOOTLEGGER

SHERIFF'S
DEPUTY

CITY
POLICE

P.W.Cromwell

Bootlegging was too widespread for law enforcement to control, as this cartoon shows.

stopped by a speakeasy, on or off duty. One speakeasy on New York's Lower East Side had entrances on two different streets. When federal agents raided and padlocked one side—which they did with regularity to show the public that they were fighting crime—they conveniently forgot to lock the other door. Customers were readmitted almost immediately, and business would continue as usual.

Police methods were questionable. Agents entrapped citizens by encouraging them to buy alcohol and arresting them when they did. They broke down doors, roughed up prisoners, planted false evidence, and conducted searches without warrants. But many officials claimed that they had to break the law to protect the law.

William (Pussyfoot) Johnson earned his nickname as a young marshal in Oklahoma—creeping up on stills in the dead of night and beating up bootleggers. He went on to edit newsletters for the Anti-Saloon League. Johnson admitted that he often lied in court in order to gain a healthy record of convictions. He bragged, "Ethics be hanged." But the public tolerated such attitudes—Johnson was fighting crime.

Excessive violence was the norm. Six federal agents once burst into the home of a suspected bootlegger, beat him up, and killed the man's wife with a shotgun blast. When asked about the woman's death, one Dry leader coldly remarked, "She was evading the law wasn't she?" In another case, this time in Kansas City, agents found some liquor buried in a backyard. Instead of digging up the bottles, they blew the cache out with dynamite. The resulting explosion damaged houses for blocks around the blast site.

Another problem was gunfire. Many government agents were unfamiliar with firearms and were sent poorly trained into the streets to fight gangsters with submachine guns, pistols, shotguns, and assorted other weaponry. Civilians were often caught in the cross fire. When an agent killed someone, even under questionable circumstances, he was usually protected from punishment because of his status as a law officer. One senator tallied up some 55 killings by federal agents in the early 1920s. Many of the dead were shot in the back—they had been running away. In other shootings, agents mistook innocent people for criminals. The supervising Bureau of Internal Revenue refused to answer questions about the deaths. Reports were often colored to make the officers look good.

The government even operated its own smuggling operations and speakeasies, supposedly to entrap gangsters. With the approval of federal judges, agents set up rum-running networks to supply clubs in New York, Peoria, and several other cities. They bought liquor in Canada, smuggled it into the United States, and sold it to bootleggers.

One of the fanciest speakeasies of the era, the Bridge Whist Club in New York, was government run. It was touted to have the best food and booze in the Big Apple—and all at taxpayers' expense. Expenditures there included $95 for an upright piano and hundreds more for the bartenders' fancy fur coats. When questioned about such luxuries, the agents who ran the place replied that they had a competitive image to uphold.

The idea behind government-managed bars was to lure the real bootleggers inside, ply them with liquor, and get them to talk about their illegal trafficking. The ruse never worked very well because, within a short time, the most powerful criminals knew what the feds were trying to do.

But the Drys kept trying. They refused to admit that their cause was a failure, arguing that the Eighteenth Amendment just needed more time to succeed. "I have not changed my mind on the question of Prohibition," said L. P. Hollis, superintendent of schools in Greenville, South Carolina, in 1925. "I should hate to think that the people of our country are willing to admit that we cannot enforce the regulations of our Constitution."

Lawrence F. Abbot, contributing editor of *The Outlook*, added that year:

> My views on the Prohibition Amendment have not changed since I wrote to you three years ago. I regard National Prohibition as a unique and important social experiment which ought to be honestly tried for a long enough period to give us the data for an intelligent judgment, either pro or con. I do not think that such a period has yet expired.

But the problems continued to grind on and on, just as the killings and law-breaking continued.

ACE AGENTS

Although some law enforcement officials "went on the take," there were many honest agents. Among them were Izzy Einstein and Moe Smith, the self-proclaimed "masters of a thousand disguises." Unlike many of his fellow officers, Einstein never carried a gun. Smith used his weapon only twice in the years he worked for the feds. Once he fired at a dog that was chasing him. The second time he shot open a door that had been slammed on his partner's arm.

Instead of rough stuff, Einstein and Smith went undercover, dressing as garbage collectors, fruit vendors, opera singers, violinists, icemen, college students, and in dozens of other getups. Their disguises generally fooled bootleggers, bartenders, drinkers, and mobsters. In an average week, the two closed and shuttered at least 15 speakeasies—once setting a record of 17 raids in one night. In one incident, the partners—along with ten other mud-smeared agents—burst into a bar dressed like football players. The agents declared that they'd just finished a winning gridiron season, and the unsuspecting bartender set up a round of free drinks. The unfortunate fellow was promptly arrested, along with everyone else in the place.

In another bust, Einstein leaned over the bar of a speakeasy and whispered to the counterman. "Did you hear the latest story?" The man replied, "No, what is it?" With a smile, the ever friendly, polite Einstein proclaimed, "You're pinched."

Over their careers, Einstein and Smith made more than 5,000 arrests and confiscated an estimated five million bottles of whiskey. Acting alone during a lightning raid to Detroit, Einstein made some 50 arrests in two

Izzy Einstein (leaning) and Moe Smith (far right) with a captured still.

days. Unfortunately, Einstein and Smith made enemies in law enforcement circles. They embarrassed other federal agents, who looked inept by comparison. As a result, the two were placed on a "hit list" and were among about 100 agents fired in a shake-up of the federal Prohibition department in New York City in 1925. Both men then went into the life insurance business and even sold policies to many of the people they had raided as agents.

Women worked on the side of the law as well. Assistant U.S. Attorney Mabel Willebrandt was called "The Scourge of Bootleggers." Willebrandt was a tough, no-nonsense lawyer appointed by President Warren Harding to head up Prohibition enforcement. She personally assigned federal raiding parties and, through her eight years as the nation's chief enforcer, was always ready to condemn drinkers.

Sheriff Laura Pratt of Macwahoc, Maine, one of few female law enforcement officers in the 1920s, was regularly called out to help capture rumrunners entering Maine from Canada. One cloudy, moonless night, a gang was spotted speeding toward Boston—they had eluded sheriffs in three towns. The angry lawmen called Pratt, warning her that a truck packed with armed toughs and a load of whiskey was on the way to Macwahoc. Ignoring their advice to deputize men to help her, Pratt leaped into her Model T and headed out to a backwoods road. When the speeding gangsters rounded a curve, there was Pratt, parked crossways in the muddy path. She jumped out with a leveled rifle and arrested the mobsters without a fight.

THE UNTOUCHABLES

Among the most famous federal agents of the Prohibition era was Eliot Ness, head of a special detachment called "The Untouchables." A young Chicagoan, Ness had been a credit company investigator before joining the Department of Justice in 1929. His experience—tirelessly checking insurance claims and credit ratings—was considered sufficient training for a Prohibition agent's job. Shortly after joining the authorities, Ness suggested forming a special group of agents who would answer to only the highest enforcement officials.

The idea of using a small, secretive team had a lot of merit. Informers were plentiful in every level of government and the police force. Raids and arrests were often thwarted when bootleggers learned about plans in advance. The fewer people who knew about a squad, Ness believed, the more effective it would be. A group of business leaders from the Chicago Association of Commerce—officially known as the Citizens' Committee but called the Secret Six—were eager to put an end to the criminal mess in Chicago. They urged the authorities to try Ness's plan.

Given the go-ahead, Ness selected nine agents, each specializing in some important task, such as electrical work or driving a car. By tapping phones, staking out gangster hideouts, and using shadowy informers such as "Willie the Whisper" and "The Clown," Ness learned exactly what the gangsters were doing, when they were doing it, and how.

Lawman Eliot Ness

The team went to work in Chicago and soon was raiding speakeasies, warehouses, and illegal breweries. Ness placed a heavy ram on the front of a truck. With some of his men guarding the rear, the roof, or other potential escape routes, the flamboyant Ness would crash through the front door of a building in his makeshift tank and take prisoners before they could flee. Stocks of confiscated liquor were destroyed.

Soon George (Red) Barker, Al Capone, and other hoods were feeling pinched by Ness's aggressive tactics. They didn't know where he would turn up next. Without reserves of alcohol to sell, bribe money grew tight. The mobs couldn't make payoffs to judges, aldermen, and other officials. The heat was on.

An angry Capone tried to buy off the squad. He dangled the tempting offer of $2,000 a week in front of each man. One by one, all ten agents refused. Two even chased a mobster's car down the road and tossed back a wad of money that he had thrown into their car. Ness took the story to the press, which immediately gave the team its famous "Untouchables" nickname.

To tweak Capone's nose, the young officer decided to drive a parade of 45 trucks—confiscated during raids on Capone's operations—past the Lexington Hotel, where the gangster was headquartered. Every truck was washed and its fenders and hubcabs were polished until they glistened. In their big black touring cars, several Untouchables led the procession, while others guarded the center and rear. To prevent word of the parade from leaking out in advance, agents from other districts were brought in at the last minute as truck drivers.

As the motorcade slowly passed, Capone's gang stared out from the upper windows of the Lexington. A number of mobsters ran outside, but the sight of heavily armed agents stopped them in their tracks. Watching his trucks roll past, Capone reportedly went into a rage, smashed furniture, and demanded that Ness be killed. The "Big Fella" was heard to say, "I want Ness dead, even if it's on the front steps of City Hall."

The mobster never got his wish. With careful legwork and background research, Ness and his crew were able to tie a net around the most colorful gangster of the era. In 1931, Capone was convicted of income tax evasion and sentenced to 11 years in prison. As a final slap to the mobster, Ness escorted him to the train station, where he was turned over to federal marshals for the long ride to jail. With Capone gone, Ness turned his attention to "Machine Gun" Jack McGurn, George (Bugs) Moran, "Tough" Tony Capezio, Frank (the Enforcer) Nitti, and other killers.

"LOUSY PUBLIC RELATIONS"

By the end of the decade, the excitement of the Roaring Twenties was fading. More and more people were repulsed as the mobsters continued their rampaging and as government corruption was exposed. President Herbert Hoover lamented "the possibility that respect for law is fading from the sensibilities of our people." It was one thing to buy a drink from the friendly neighborhood bootlegger and quite another to have bullet-riddled bodies turn up in hometown ditches. The gangsters' glamorous image became more and more tarnished as their misdeeds grew.

The St. Valentine's Day Massacre has been called a major turning point. On February 14, 1929, two hired killers from St. Louis—dressed as police officers—and three members of Capone's mob strolled into the warehouse headquarters of Bugs Moran in Chicago. Moran and one of his friends saw the group coming and quickly left the scene. They were lucky. Inside, seven of Moran's men probably thought they were facing a typical police raid. But they were mowed down with machine-gun fire. The killers left quietly; the bogus cops holding guns on Capone's gangsters to make the shoot-out look real. The slaughter demonstrated the ruthlessness of the mobsters. It was "lousy public relations" admitted one gangster.

A new era was dawning. Since the Wets could point out that much of the country's crime and corruption was caused by Prohibition, their cause became more respectable. In the House and Senate, a contingent of Wets banded together to consider reforms, perhaps even making beer and wine legal again.

More and more people were moving from the country to the city to find work, a migration that undercut rural support for the Anti-Saloon League. When Wayne Wheeler died of a heart attack in 1927, the Dry

The St. Valentine's Day Massacre shocked the American public.

movement lost its primary spokesperson. His successors frightened people when they said that jazz music and dancing should also be banned.

Herbert Hoover, elected in 1928 as a Republican Dry, set about trying to make Prohibition work. He established the Wickersham Commission, charged with recommending ways to improve enforcement of the Eighteenth Amendment. But a majority of the commission questioned whether the amendment could be enforced at all. Some members suggested that Prohibition be put to a new national vote.

That response surprised Hoover. But he disregarded many of the commission's recommendations. He issued what he said was a summary of the group's findings, stating in his report that antidrinking laws needed to be more strictly enforced. When the media revealed that Hoover had misrepresented the commission's conclusions, some people reacted with anger. Others, like Franklin P. Adams, writing in the *New York World,* responded with satire:

> Prohibition is an awful flop.
>   We like it.
> It can't stop what it's meant to stop.
>   We like it.
> It's left a trail of graft and slime,
> It don't prohibit worth a dime,
> It's filled our land with vice and crime.
>   Nevertheless, we're for it.

Within a year, donations to the Anti-Saloon League tumbled to half their previous level.

By then, even some of the most ardent Dry enforcers were getting out of the battle. Assistant U.S. Attorney Mabel Willebrandt resigned in 1929 to become legal counsel for Fruit Industries, Inc., a group of California wine-grape growers. When the group developed and marketed a grape concentrate with a 12 percent alcohol content, Willebrandt even convinced government officials that the product did not violate Prohibition laws.

The pendulum was swinging in the Wets' direction. Too many questions had surfaced about the moral, legal, and ethical value of keeping Prohibition on the books.

THE LOST WAR

Public questions of great moment, on which the stability of our government depends, are pressing for solution. But around them all we find contained the long tentacles of this Octopus— Prohibition.

—Congresswoman Florence Kahn
on the Great Depression

Pﬂresident Hoover took very seriously his role in administering the Volstead Act. Between 1929 and 1932, he doubled the number of people imprisoned on the federal level for liquor violations. Hoover emphasized that if a law was wrong, "its rigid enforcement is the surest guaranty of its repeal." He added, "If it is right, its enforcement is the quickest method of compelling respect for it."

But total enforcement never came about. The federal government did not take full responsibility for making sure Prohibition worked. It depended on cities and states to provide the necessary money and labor. But most local governments, although they might have initially supported Prohibition, never had enough time, resources, or energy to wholeheartedly back up the law.

"BROTHER, CAN YOU SPARE A DIME?"

Another major reason for the failure of Prohibition, especially by the late 1920s, was the economy. During the 1920s, many Americans spent more than they earned, borrowing money to buy stocks and bonds in an uncontrolled frenzy of speculation. On "Black Tuesday," October 29, 1929, the stock market collapsed. Investors lost vast amounts of money. Businesses closed. Banks failed. Debts went unpaid. Millions of Americans lost their savings. Millions lost their jobs.

The stock market crash marked the beginning of the Great Depression. Soon Americans were much more concerned about finding work, keeping their jobs, and feeding their families than about Prohibition and gangsters. People continued drinking, perhaps to forget their misery. In 1930, the Prohibition Bureau estimated that an average of seven gallons of liquor was being drunk each year for every person in the United States.

Although thousands of illegal stills and distilleries were seized and more than 90,000 bootleggers arrested and fined in 1931, these efforts hardly made a dent in the liquor traffic. Police said that they could catch only about a quarter of the people involved. One officer estimated that 10 percent of the American population was engaged in the illicit liquor business—from speakeasy bartenders to gun-toting racketeers to druggists who filled false prescriptions for medicinal alcohol. Indeed, as the

President Hoover stepped up Prohibition efforts.

country staggered through the Depression years, bootlegging and rum-running were often a means of survival.

Adding to the misery, drought hit the midwestern and plains states in the early 1930s. Dust storms blackened the sky for days. Crops failed, and thousands of poor farmers were bankrupted. Leaving behind their homes in Oklahoma and other "Dust Bowl" states, "Okies" filled the roads in rickety Model T autos and sagging trucks, searching for work and a better life in California or elsewhere.

There seemed to be no end of grief. By 1932, more than 12 million Americans were out of work in a nation of 130 million people. Families did what they could to survive. Depending on handouts, tens of thousands lived in shantytowns named—after the president—Hoovervilles.

BLAMING PROHIBITION

A call for the repeal of Prohibition grew louder. Wets claimed that Prohibition had caused the Depression, and it was difficult to prove otherwise. Economists pointed out that the government was losing more than $500 million a year by not being able to tax a legal brewing and distilling industry. Much of that money went to gangsters and corrupt politicians instead. Wets also claimed that a legal alcohol industry would result in more jobs.

The Drys had promised a better life with Prohibition, but they had failed to deliver. Humorist Will Rogers wrote in 1931:

> What does Prohibition amount to, if your neighbor's children are not eating? It's food, not drink, is our problem now. We were so afraid that the poor people might drink, now we fixed it so they can't eat. The working classes didn't bring this one, it was the big boys that thought the financial drunk was going to last forever.

Not all of America's woes could be traced to Prohibition. But leading Wets argued that life would be wonderful with repeal. Their extravagant claims echoed those used by Drys years earlier. The attacks on Prohibition were strong enough to force the Drys to consider a compromise.

Some Drys said they would approve the sale of wine and beer if taverns remained outlawed. But others still clung to a belief in Prohibition. "There is as much a chance of repealing the Eighteenth Amendment as there is for a hummingbird to fly to Mars with the Washington Monument tied to its tail," said Senator Morris Sheppard in 1930.

Meanwhile, a leading prohibitionist, Bishop James A. Cannon, was caught in a financial and sex scandal, an incident that helped discredit the entire Dry movement. Although Cannon was never convicted of any crime, the scandal knocked him from leadership within the Prohibition movement. Few people still believed that Drys upheld the banner of moral behavior.

For a time, Drys had hoped that the passage of the Nineteenth Amendment, which had granted the vote to women, would consolidate their hold on the country. Drys figured that politically active women, such as those who belonged to the Women's Christian Temperance Union, would continue to crusade against drinking. But, by the early 1930s, many women were discouraged and upset by the shaky economic, moral, and criminal state of the nation.

The hungry and homeless line up for relief packages in Depression-era Washington, D.C.

The Women's Organization for National Prohibition Reform enrolls supporters in Chicago.

Pauline Sabin, former president of the Women's National Republican Club, caused an explosion of gossip and concern when she resigned her office and took up the Wet cause. Poised, wealthy, and well connected, Sabin gathered more than 300,000 members to her Women's Organization for National Prohibition Reform. Chapters were founded in almost every state and in the District of Columbia. The women were educated, politically savvy, and eager to help candidates who supported their cause. They knew exactly what they wanted: repeal of Prohibition.

THE FAILED EXPERIMENT

The presidential conventions of 1932 brought the Prohibition issue to a head. Both parties met in Chicago: the Republicans early in June and the Democrats at the end of the month. When a reporter wrote that many leading Republican delegates were visiting a speakeasy across the street from the convention hall, the police raided the place. Everyone was released, however, and a few delegates were even directed to other neighborhood bars by friendly cops.

The top Democratic contender for the nomination was Franklin D. Roosevelt, a reformist governor of New York. Initially dependent on rural support that was primarily Dry, Roosevelt eventually came out in favor of repeal as one means of solving the nation's economic problems. After a flurry of arguments on the convention floor and much backroom politicking, the Democrats went on record as opposing Prohibition and supporting its repeal. After heated debate, they backed Roosevelt as their candidate.

Herbert Hoover was renominated by the Republicans. The Republican platform didn't out-and-out support repeal, but it did call for resubmitting Prohibition to a vote of the states. Charismatic and friendly, and promoting a program of economic reforms known as the New Deal, Roosevelt swept the national vote in a landslide. Wet candidates, primarily Democratic but also a fair number of Republicans, also won congressional offices.

Resolutions supporting repeal of the Eighteenth Amendment were quickly introduced in the House and Senate. They passed overwhelmingly. After much discussion, the proposed Twenty-first Amendment won support. The key passage read simply: "The Eighteenth Article of Amendment to the Constitution of the United States is hereby repealed." The second passage promised to help uphold liquor laws in states that chose to remain Dry. "It was about time to wipe the slate clean and start over," wrote historian John D. Hicks.

States were told to hold conventions to ratify the new amendment. In anticipation of repeal, Roosevelt began laying off enforcement agents shortly after taking office in March 1933. Next, at Roosevelt's urging, Congress modified the Volstead Act. As of April 7, intoxicating liquor was redefined as any drink containing more than 3.2 percent alcohol. Now 3.2 beer—almost as strong as the real stuff—was legal.

The celebration began. In St. Louis, Anheuser-Busch had almost

30,000 barrels of beer ready to roll. A colorful cavalcade of trucks took the appreciated brew to taverns around the city, where thirsty and happy drinkers waited. In Milwaukee, the "Beer Capital of America," snow was falling heavily. But three long lines of people waited outside each of the seven breweries that had been making soda pop and near beer. In one line, folks waited to buy cases of beer; in the second line, they waited to receive a free glass of suds (at least 15,000 drinks were eventually poured); and in the third line, hundreds waited patiently for new brewing jobs.

At 12:01 A.M. on April 7, every factory whistle in town blasted away, church bells pealed, and crowds roared. Twenty-three minutes later, despite the snowstorm, a plane took off for Washington with a load of beer for President Roosevelt. On April 17, Milwaukee held its official celebration, with 20,000 folks inside an auditorium and thousands more on

Near beer is dead!

the streets. Six bands played as everyone roared, "Ein Prosit!" the German phrase for "a toast."

On April 10, 1933, Michigan was the first state to officially ratify the Twenty-first amendment. On December 5, Utah became the deciding 36th state to approve it. Although a few states chose to remain Dry (Kentucky, Kansas, Oklahoma, and Mississippi), national Prohibition was officially dead.

For the benefit of movie newsreel cameras, Acting Secretary of State William Phillips read the repeal proclamation. Revelers hit the streets again. But this time the victory was not even as boisterous as many New Year's Eve celebrations. Since the Utah vote had taken place late in the day, many speakeasies, even those that had managed to get the proper license beforehand, did not have enough alcohol on hand. A sign high over Billy Minsky's dance hall in New York flashed, "We'll Take Gin." One joker complained that it was easier to get a drink when Prohibition was in force.

Those lucky enough to find a drink toasted the demise of the Eighteenth Amendment. Many speakeasies cut their prices 40 to 60 percent in celebration. The unofficial bootlegger for the Maryland legislature, sorrowfully making his last delivery to the lawmakers, was told by a police officer, "It's all over. You can leave now." In various cities, straw-packed dummies labeled "Prohibition" were burned in raging bonfires or hung from street lamps. An American Legion post in Freeport, Long Island, put a dummy against a wall, formed a firing squad, and shot it.

PROHIBITION'S LEGACY

The repeal of Prohibition did not save the United States from the Great Depression as some had hoped. Americans continued to struggle with joblessness and hunger until the early 1940s, when the defense buildup of World War II finally revived the nation's economy.

But the fallout from Prohibition was considerable. One legacy was the vast influx of money into the hands of criminals. This pool of funds allowed gangsters to gain control of prostitution, gambling, drug dealing, and other illegal activities. The cash also enabled gangsters to move into

***The first shipment of legal gin leaves Philadelphia for San Francisco,
October 23, 1933.***

legitimate businesses, through which they "laundered" money, making it
look honestly earned. Dry cleaning and restaurant supply firms were often targeted for takeover. Many labor unions also fell under gangsters'
control. It took years of effort by the authorities to root the criminals out.

But ghosts of rumrunners and bootleggers remained. In 1957, plank-
ing and part of the cargo from the *Maude,* a sunken Canadian tug, were
recovered off Detroit's West Grand Boulevard. The ship had sunk in

1923 with a load of smuggled beer. Workers who found the ship opened a 34-year-old bottle and enjoyed a sample.

Although many of the gangland hotels, speakeasies, illegal breweries, and shootout sites from the 1920s and 1930s long ago fell under the wrecker's ball, Prohibition still lives on—in gangster movies, museums, and *The Untouchables* reruns on television. People can visit Al Capone's Wisconsin getaway near Couderay—complete with a guntower and eight-car garage—and take "Gangster Tours" in cities like Chicago, St. Paul, and Milwaukee. From downtown Detroit, visitors can scan the Detroit River, where rumrunners plied their trade. To the south, in Windsor, Ontario, stands a huge Canadian Club whiskey sign marking the Hiram Walker distillery, which did a thriving business during Prohibition days.

The Prohibition debate has even resurfaced in regard to modern-day drug use. Some people think that drug trafficking would fall off and that crime would decrease if drugs were legalized and regulated by the government. Many people fiercely oppose legalizing drugs. Yet a few prominent politicians have backed the idea, pointing to the failure and lawlessness of Prohibition to press home their point.

Most people agree that America's "noble experiment," as President Hoover called Prohibition, was indeed a failure. Across the nation, there was a sense of relief when America's long drought was over. This feeling might best be summarized by a drinker who slipped up to the bar in Heine's, a Milwaukee hot spot that had just reopened in 1933. Asked if he was ready for a beer, he answered: "Yes, please. Make mine legal."

SELECTED BIBLIOGRAPHY

Asbury, Herbert. *The Great Illusion: An Informal History of Prohibition.* New York: Doubleday & Company, Inc., 1950.

Babson, Steve. *Working Detroit.* New York: Adama Books, 1984.

Blocker, Jack S., Jr. *American Temperance Movements: Cycles of Reform.* Boston: Twayne Publishers, 1989.

Burlingame, Roger. *Henry Ford.* New York: Alfred A. Knopf, 1955.

Burns, Roger. *Preacher Billy Sunday and Big-Time American Evangelism.* New York: W. W. Norton, 1992.

Dorr, Rheta. *Drink: Coercion or Control?* New York: Frederick A. Staves Publishing Co., 1929.

Cashman, Sean Dennis. *Prohibition: The Lie of the Land.* New York: Macmillan Publishing Co., 1981.

Clark, Norman. *The Dry Years: Prohibition and Social Changes in Washington.* Seattle: University of Washington Press, 1965.

Conley, Paul C., and Andrew A. Sorensen. *The Staggering Steeple: The Story of Alcoholism and the Churches.* Philadelphia: A Pilgrim Press Book, 1971.

Dorsett, Lyle W. *Billy Sunday and the Redemption of Urban America.* New York: W. B. Erdmans Press, 1991.

Engelmann, Larry. *Intemperance: The Lost War against Liquor.* New York: The Free Press, 1979.

Franklin, Jimmy Lewis. *Born Sober: Prohibition in Oklahoma, 1907–1959.* Norman: University of Oklahoma Press, 1971.

Geldeman, Carol. *Henry Ford: The Wayward Capitalist.* New York: Dial Press, 1981.

Goldston, Robert. *The Great Depression: The United States in the Thirties.* Indianapolis: The Bobbs-Merrill Co., 1968.

Kobler, James. *Ardent Spirits: The Rise and Fall of Prohibition.* New York: G. P. Putnam's Sons, 1973.

Lee, Henry. *How Dry We Were: Prohibition Revisited.* Englewood Cliffs, N.J.: Prentice-Hall, 1963.

McElvaine, Robert S. *The Great Depression: America, 1929–1941.* New York: Times Books, 1984.

McLoughlin, William G. *Billy Sunday Was His Real Name.* Chicago: University of Chicago Press, 1958.

Mordden, Ethan. *That Jazz! An Idiosyncratic Social History of the American Twenties.* New York: G. P. Putnam's Sons, 1978.

Ness, Eliot, and Oscar Fraley. *The Untouchables.* Mattituck, N.Y.: The American Reprint Co., 1976.

Parrish, Michael E. *Anxious Decades: America in Prosperity and Depression, 1920–1941.* New York: W. W. Norton & Co., 1992.

Stelzle, Charles. *Why Prohibition!* New York: George H. Doran Company, 1918.

Vecki, Victor G. *Alcohol and Prohibition.* Philadelphia: J. B. Lippincott Company, 1923.

Wells, Robert W. *This Is Milwaukee: A Colorful Portrait of the City That Made Beer Famous.* New York: Doubleday & Company, 1970.

INDEX

ACKNOWLEDGMENTS

Photographs and illustrations used with permission of The Bettmann Archive: pp. 2, 7, 8, 11, 33, 41 (top), 42, 52, 54; Library of Congress: pp. 6, 12, 14, 16, 17, 18, 25, 26, 32 (both), 59, 74, 75, 78; UPI/Bettmann: pp. 20, 34, 36, 41 (bottom), 45, 47, 62, 63, 67, 69, 72, 80, 82, 88; Michigan Historical Collections, Bentley Historical Library, University of Michigan: pp. 21, 23, 28, 29, 30, 58, 64; State Photographic Archives, Stozier Library, Florida State Library: p. 39; U.S.I.A., National Archives, Photo No. 306-NT-163820C: p. 44; Illinois State Historical Library: p. 48; Hollywood Book and Poster: p. 50; *TV Times:* p. 57; Missouri Historical Society, St. Louis: pp. 60, 61; U.S. Office of War Information, Photo No. 306-NT-163-554C: p. 77.

Front cover: UPI/Bettmann (left); Library of Congress (center); Kansas State Historical Society, Topeka (right)
Back cover: The Bettmann Archive

Time for a drink; Philadelphians toast repeal.

DATE DUE